Wherever you tread, the blushing flowers shall rise,
and all things flourish where you turn your eyes.

Alexander Pope

One might say of me that in this book,
I have only made up a bouquet of other people's
flowers, and that of my own, I have only
provided the string that ties them together.

Michel Montaigne

FLOWERING VINES

Mandevilla *(Mandevilla splendens)*

The flowers of most plants do not grow larger after their buds open, but Mandevilla flowers are only about half-size when they open. They reach their maximum size and richest color several days later. The namesake of this flower was H. J. Mandeville, a British minister in Buenos Aires in the 1800's. Mandeville is sometimes called Pink Allamanda. It is not very closely related to the Allamanda vine, but is in the same family.

Fascination with Vines

Vines are more numerous in tropical areas where the growth of trees and other vegetation is very dense. In this environment, vines are very well equipped to compete for light.

"Vining" is a truly cunning stategy in this life and death struggle among plants. Vines do not need to put their energy into building heavy stems and trunks. Thus, they can use their extra growth resources to quickly lengthen their stems. Through various climbing techniques, they make use of other plants to reach the light at the top of the forest in a fraction of the time required by their competitors. Once the sunlight strikes the vine, resources are used to produce more foliage for food production and for further expansion.

Here are the four ways to the top. Some vines climb with rootlets that produce adhesive disks and literally glue the vine to its support. Some climb by twining, or wrapping their stems around the support (some species are known to twist in one direction only). A third climbing technique is the use of tendrils, small grasping "hands" that vines produce at the tips of their leaves or from their stems. A final method is "scrambling" by shooting out long, arching stems which loop over other plants. Many scrambling vines have thorns which help them to hold on while clambering over the "back" of the other plant.

Not all vines climb. Technically, a vine is a plant which cannot grow up without support. But, some vines are content to merely creep along the ground without ever rising.

Wax Plant *(Hoya carnosa)*

This beautiful vine produces ball-shaped clusters of flowers. The flowers of each cluster all radiate from a small spur on the stem. This same spur will produce more flowers the following year.

Each flower is a star-shape within a star. Sometimes the flower cluster will take the form of a complete ball and encircle the main stem as in the photo at right.

The flowers are fragrant and long lasting. Because of the shiny appearance of the petals, *Hoya* has also been called Porcelain Flower. Another common name is Honey Plant because of the small drops of honey-like liquid that often drip from the flowers.

This vine can be planted on the trunk of a palm and it can thrive without much care. It is tough enough to survive the occasional frosts which sometimes strike Florida.

Hoya was named for Thomas Hoy, the chief gardener of an English Duke. It is native from China to Australia.

Queen's Wreath *(Petrea volubilis)*

Native to tropical America, this vine produces foot-long showpieces of color and lacy texture. The true flowers last only a day or two, but when they drop, the five-pointed, star-shaped calyxes remain and there may be as many as 30 or 40 in each group.

The stems of older vines may become thick enough to be almost tree-like and self-supporting. The leaves are so rough textured that the plant is sometimes called the Sandpaper Vine.

The Latin name honors Lady Petre, a patron of botanists and wife of one of the British governors of India.

Rubber Vine *(Cryptostegia grandiflora)*

Rubber Vine has a milky sap. A close relative was considered as a possible source of rubber during World War II because it thrives in the Caribbean. All parts are poisonous and can be a hazard to grazing cattle. It is native to Madagascar.

Allamanda *(Allamanda cathartica)*

In the Hawaiian language, this common tropical flower is given the grandiose title of Heavenly Chief.

Allamanda has no tendrils. It climbs by scrambling and leaning. Gardeners must provide some ties or supports.

In nature this plant grows through and upon another plant. It throws out long, arching shoots, similar to Bougainvillea, but if nothing provides support, they will just droop down to the ground. It is a native of Brazil.

Mexican Flame Vine
(Senecio confusus)

A "genus" is a group of closely related species. This particular genus, *Senecio,* is one of the largest groups of plants, containing over 2000 species. *Senecio* contains a lot of variety including annuals and even some succulents.

This particular plant is native to Mexico.

Bougainvillea (Bougainvillea hybrids)

This Brazilian vine has tall, arching shoots, and is much admired for its showy colors. The most exciting parts are the gaudy, papery leaves (called "bracts") which surround the tiny white flowers with a three-sided, protective enclosure.

In the photo above, one of the flowers has been torn open, perhaps by an insect, revealing the tiny stamens inside.

The plant is named after Louis de Bougainville, a French scientist, lawyer, and explorer whose name also graces an island in the South Pacific. Bougainvillea is one of the best known plants of the tropics.

Bridal Bouquet *(Stephanotis floribunda)*

This vine is a native of Madagascar which has very fragrant flowers. *Stephanotis* was popular in Florida for bridal bouquets until the cost of the handwork in wiring all the tiny flowers made the price prohibitive.

Stephanotis flowers have a mild fragrance that is appreciated by people who find stronger perfumes a bit overwhelming and seek more subtle pleasures.

Rangoon Creeper *(Quisqualis indica)*

The flowers are white when they open and gradually change color to pink, and then red. The blossoms are very fragrant at night.

It was given the name *"Quisqualis"* which means "Who, what?" in Latin, by a botanist who was amazed at seeing the plant transform itself from a self-supporting shrub, which he had planted in his yard, into a climbing vine. The Rangoon Creeper sent a runner over to a neighboring tree and began climbing the tree. The shrubby part of the plant then died, leaving behind a climbing vine.

Gloriosa Lily *(Gloriosa* spp.*)* [*]

The petals of this flower point downward in the bud stage, but when the flower opens, the petals are pointing straight up.

Another unusual feature is that the stamens are spread out in a circle resembling the face of a clock with the pistil pointing like one of the sweep hands.

This vine climbs by means of tendrils at the tip of each leaf.

After the vine blooms, it dies and a new vine starts growing from the root tuber.

Loofa *(Luffa aegyptiaca)*

This vine, in addition to having beautiful flowers, produces long gourds. These are processed to remove all the flesh from the fiber, creating the famous "loofa sponge" which is widely sold for scrubbing the skin and to help improve the complexion.

[*] The abbreviation "spp." means "various species" and is used in this book when more than one species of a plant is grown in Florida and when it would be beyond the scope of this book to discuss all these species.

Chalice Vine *(Solandra* spp.*)*

It is said that the very large flowers of this plant are silver in color at the time the buds open and that they change to gold in a few days. This may be an exaggeration. The new flowers are a light yellow color and later become a much deeper golden hue.

The huge buds of the Chalice Vine open very rapidly and some claim that it is possible to actually see the movement.

A native of Mexico, Chalice Vine is also known as the Cup of Gold.

Flame Vine *(Pyrostegia venusta)*

This Brazilian vine is capable of covering large areas such as walls, fences, and even the roofs of buildings with a thick carpet of the most brilliant orange color.

The Latin name means "fire on the roof," but this refers to the color of the upper lip of the tubular flowers or the "roof" of the flower, and not to the fact that the vine sometimes grows on the roofs of buildings.

Honeysuckle Vine *(Lonicera japonica)*

The blossoms form in distinctive pairs and turn from white to yellow before wilting. These flowers are important for their medical properties in China and other parts of Asia where this plant is native.

Trumpet Honeysuckle
(Lonicera sempervirens)

This Florida native plant is also called Coral Honeysuckle. It is interesting to notice that it has two opposite leaves fused together just below the flower cluster. The other leaves of the plant are not connected to each other in this manner. This is a feature common to many different honeysuckles.

Passion Flower *(Passiflora* spp.*)*
The Legend of the Passion Flower

Early Spanish explorers saw religious symbolism in the amazing flowers of this vine. It was called Passion Flower as it suggested to them the Passion of Christ.

In the red species, the color symbolized the blood shed on the cross; the ten petals and sepals represented the ten apostles present at the crucifixion; the five stamens the five wounds; the three styles the three nails (or, in some versions, Christ and the two thieves who were crucified with him); the vine tendrils the ropes and scourges; the three secondary leaf bracts the holy trinity. In the white and blue flower, the white symbolizes purity and the blue the heaven above. The flower is usually open three days representing the three years of Christ's ministry on earth.

The Jesuit priests who saw natives of the New World eating the fruit of the Passion Flower took it as a sign that they were hungry for Christianity. On a more secular level, the fruits are very popular in many parts of the world for making juice.

11

Coral Vine *(Antigonon leptopus)*

These flowers resemble a string of small hearts, hence the romantic common name, Chain of Love. In its native country of Mexico the underground tubers are used as food.

Bleeding Heart
(Clerodendrum thomsoniae)

The stamens extend far beyond the petals and seem to beckon. This feature made the flowers useful in Malaysian witchcraft when attracting something was desired.

The bottom photos show a hybrid of Bleeding Heart called The Java Glory Bean. After the flowers drop, the attractive calyxes remain on the plant.

Legend of the Bleeding Heart Vine

A beautiful woman was deserted by her lover. When the young man later returned to search for her, she could not be found. But, on the spot where they had quarreled and her tears had touched the ground, a flower was blooming. The shape of its blossoms resembled a bleeding heart.

Night Blooming Cereus
(Selenicereus spp.*)*

Night Blooming Cereus is a Mexican cactus in the form of a climbing vine with stiff stems and tiny thorns. Its flowers are among the most spectacular anywhere. They start opening just after dark and are fully open several hours later. With the first light of dawn they start to wilt and are gone forever.

Each plant has one night of the year when most of its blooms open. There will be several other nights with just a few blooms. Look for these flowers in the middle of summer.

Chinese will not marry when this flower is blooming. It is regarded as a bad omen for a stable marriage because of the very transitory nature of the blossoms. Nevertheless, nature lovers in China hold parties for viewing the flowers, the same as people in Florida. Other common names include Queen of the Night and Rope Cactus.

The photo at far right shows the new flower buds and the photo, near right, the ripening fruit several weeks

Sex and the Father of Botany

The Latin name *Thunbergia* honors Carl Thunberg, a colleague of Linnaeus. Linnaeus was a Swedish physician and scientist regarded as the "Father of Botany" for his creation of the first modern classification system for plants.

With all this classifying going on, Linnaeus had plenty of chances to honor his friends and associates. He enshrined them left and right, but reserved only one small flower for his own name, "a plant of Lappland, lowly, insignificant, disregarded, flowering but for a brief space – from Linnaeus who resembles it."

Linnaeus was much absorbed with the fact that flowers are, basically, sex organs. He wrote "The genitalia of plants we regard with delight; of animals with abomination; and of ourselves with strange thoughts."

He described flower petals as "bridal beds which the Creator has so gloriously arranged, adorned with such noble bed curtains and perfumed with so many sweet scents that the bride-groom may celebrate his nuptials with his bride with all the greater solemnity."

Linnaeus was the first to investigate plant ecology, describe food chains, and study habitats. Casting aside all false modesty he declared, justifiably, that he had "done more to change botany than anyone in history."

Sky Vine *(Thunbergia grandiflora)*

A native of India, it blooms all year long, with large, sky-blue flowers. The leaves are used in Malay folk medicine.

King's Mantle *(Thunbergia erecta)*

This African *Thunbergia* is not a vine, but a bushy shrub. Another common name for this plant is Monarch's Robe.

Trumpet Creeper (*Campsis radicans*)

Small children sometimes put one blossom over each finger and wave the bloody-looking hand menacingly, shouting "Witch's fingers!" It is native to the eastern part of the U.S. and grows as far north as Massachusetts.

All species of Trumpet Creeper vines have stamens that are enclosed rather than protruding from the tubular part of the flower. This distinguishes Trumpet Creepers from a number of similar vines. Another characteristic is that each blossom has five lobes and three of these are larger than the other two.

Pelican Flower
(*Aristolochia grandiflora*)

This flower is grown as a novelty in Florida because of the amazing resemblance of its immature flowers to the shape of that most popular bird, the Brown Pelican.

This flower also has a fascinating insect trap described more fully in this book under Dutchman's Pipe, another flower of the same genus. It is native to Central America.

Star Jasmine *(Jasminum nitidum)*

This scrambling vine is often trained as a shrub. It is a native of the Admiralty Islands which are located in the South Pacific to the north of Australia.

The star-shaped flowers are very fragrant. A close relative of this species is used in the manufacture of perfume and is widely cultivated in both India and China.

Confederate Jasmine
(Trachelospermum jasminoides)

This is one of the most common among those Florida plants which are called Jasmine. It climbs high without tendrils by wrapping itself around a support.

Many people think "Confederate" refers to the American Confederacy, but the name derives from the confederacy of the Malay Sultanates, joined together by the British in the 1800's.

White, tubular, fragrant flowers, such as Confederate Jasmine, are usually pollinated by beetles. These creatures may be nocturnal and entirely dependent on their sense of smell to reach the flowers.

<u>All about</u> Jasmine

As a common name, Jasmine refers to many small, sweet-scented flowers. Of the following types, only Star Jasmine and Yellow Primrose Jasmine actually belong to the genus *Jasminum*. Jasmine has been spelled "Jessamin" or "Jessamine" by some writers to distinguish Jasmine-like white flowers from the true Jasmines. The distinction is no longer clear and the various spellings are now used interchangeably for the common names.

At one time it was fashionable to call anything with a strong smell "Jasmine." The goat in the TV "Our Gang" comedy was named Jasmine.

Night Blooming Jasmine
(Cestrum nocturnum)

This plant is not a vine, but a scrambling shrub. It blooms several times during the year and is astoundingly fragrant. The flowers, which only open at night, can be noticed from as far as several blocks away by the heavy scent of their perfume.

Some people love the fragrance and others find it oppressive and overpowering, reminiscent of a funeral parlor. The berries and sap are poisonous and sensitive people may even find the fragrance mildly narcotic.

Primrose Jasmine (Jasminum mesnyi)

Also called Yellow Jasmine, it is native to China. The blossoms form gently curving "waterfalls" of color.

FLOWERING PLANTS

Hibiscus *(Hibiscus rosa-sinensis* cultivars*)*

Hibiscus originated in China, India, and the Pacific islands. It was first brought to the West in the 1600's. Through hybridization, more than 4,000 varieties have been created over the years. Perhaps 500 varieties still exist in the world today.

The popularity of flower styles changes like clothing fashions, so that, of the new strains that are developed, not all are perpetuated. But new Hibiscus varieties are still desired and the members of numerous Hibiscus societies hold exhibitions to show off their latest creations.

The Hibiscus is the national flower of Malaysia, the state flower of Hawaii, and one of the most well known features of tropical places around the world. It is so popular in so many countries it has even been called the tropical equivalent of the Rose.

Hibiscus flowers are generally one-day blooms. They open in the morning and close in the evening. A nice feature is that cut Hibiscus flowers will usually stay fresh for the entire day, even without water.

This is one reason they are popular with young ladies in the Pacific islands who wish to adorn their hair. In Tahiti it is traditional that a Hibiscus worn on one side of the head indicates marital commitment and the opposite when worn on the other side.

The petals of red Hibiscus flowers, when crushed, yield a purple dye that is used as shoe polish in India. For this reason, they are not used in Hawaiian leis as they will stain the clothing underneath if pressed.

The so-called "Tree Hibiscus" is usually an ordinary Hibiscus that has been trained to grow as a tree through careful pruning. Such a plant is called a "standard" in nursery trade jargon. However, Montezuma's Hibiscus, and several others are actually trees.

Oleander *(Nerium oleander)*

The Oleander thrives under difficult conditions. It can be grown in the presence of salt spray on the beaches and in the polluted air along heavily travelled highways. Its abundant blooms are spectacular in the spring and summer, but it is dangerous. It has been planted along causeways and beaches even though all parts of the plant are quite poisonous. People who use its branches for cooking marshmallows and hotdogs risk serious consequences as the sap and even the smoke from the burning leaves is poisonous.

The Oleander grows abundantly in the Holy Land, especially around fresh water streams. For this reason it is thought to be the "Rose" of the Bible mentioned in Ecclesiasticus 24:14, 39:13. (Ecclesiasticus, or Sirach, is a book of the Apochrypha found in Catholic bibles).

Thryallis *(Galphimia glauca)*

Also known as the Shower of Gold, this plant is very popular for landscaping because it is covered with flowers most of the year. It is native to Mexico.

Crape Myrtle (*Lagerstroemia indica*)

Crape Myrtle is a flowering shrub from China. It can become tall and tree-like.

The name is sometimes spelled "Crepe," a reference to the crinkled flower petals. The flowers range in color from white through pink to lavender and reddish purple.

Angel's Trumpet (*Brugmansia* spp.)

You will hear the angel's trumpet blowing if you eat this flower or its seeds because it is highly poisonous. The unfortunate part is that these beautiful flowers would be naturally tempting for a small child to pick and place in his mouth like a horn.

The fact that the flowers face downward has inspired a variety of common names in various languages. Such names usually translate loosely as "ground-gazing flower."

Smoking Datura leaves, although a dangerous practice, was an old folk remedy for asthma. The plant has also been abused in various ways as a hallucinogenic drug.

Bird-of-Paradise *(Strelitzia reginae)*

These unique flowers have suggested to some the form of a bird in flight and to others the plumed head of a bird. However fanciful these thoughts may be, at least it is true that the flowers are pollinated by birds.

The blossoms are packed together in a green protective sheath. They emerge one at a time over a period of several days so that the flower cluster gradually grows larger and more showy. Each individual blossom has three orange petals and one blue "petal" which is actually a modified stamen.

The Bird-of-Paradise is a member of the banana family. Plants of this group are not shrubs because they lack woody stems.

White Bird-of-Paradise
(Strelitzia nicolai)

This plant is a close relative of the Bird-of-Paradise, but more tree-like. It can reach a height of 30 feet and has a stem that looks very much like a tree trunk. The flowers are similar to the Bird-of-Paradise, but they are blue and white in color and lack the long stems.

Glorybower *(Clerodendrum splendens)*
    This native of tropical Africa is very common among the summer flowers of Florida. The colorful berries are just as attractive as the blossoms. Another common name for this plant is Bag Flower.

Chinese Hat Plant
(Holmskioldia sanguinea)

The unique shape of the flowers has inspired the common names Mandarin Cap, and the Cup and Saucer Plant. The flowers grow directly on the branches rather than having their own little stems.

The long tube in the center of the flowers is composed of flower petals joined together. When the petals drop, the calyx remains, forming the hat shape.

Chinese Hat Plant is native to the Himalayan region of Asia.

Princess Flower *(Tibouchina urvilleana)*

This flower features unusually rich color. It has been called the Brazilian Spiderflower because the unusual sickle-shaped anthers and their stalks look like the legs of a spider.

Some species of *Tibouchina* can grow very large and tree-like. These flowers are native to Brazil.

Shrimp Plant *(Justicia brandegeana)*

The blossoms of this plant bear such a resemblance to boiled shrimp that the common name in almost every language includes the word "shrimp."

It is interesting to note that the most colorful parts are the orange bracts. The actual flowers are small white structures.

The Shrimp Plant grows wild along the roadsides in Mexico where it is native.

Red Bauhinia *(Bauhinia punctata)*

This sprawling shrub comes from the region of the Cape of Good Hope, Africa. It is sometimes known as Pride of the Cape.

The brick-red flowers resemble Nasturtiums that have grown very large.

In Florida Red Bauhinia blooms almost all summer.

Plumbago *(Plumbago auriculata)*

The name Plumbago comes from the Latin word for lead. This South African plant was once used to treat lead poisoning.

In Africa, a powder of the charred roots is rubbed into cuts in the skin to produce the decorative welts so admired by some tribes.

The flower has interesting, hairy buds. These hairs are sticky and persist after the flower has bloomed. They help disperse the seeds by causing them to stick to anything touching the plant.

Flowers that are really blue in color, like the Plumbago, are relatively uncommon. For example, among the thousands of hybrid Hibiscus, there are no truly blue flowers although people have been trying to breed them for many years.

Chenille Plant *(Acalypha hispida)*

This native of Asia is grown for its long colorful bloom spikes which are covered with hundreds of tiny male flowers. These flowers have red stamens which produce the velvety effect, but have no petals. The female flowers are inconspicuous.

Candlebush *(Cassia alata)*

The flower clusters shown in the photo are made up mostly of unopened buds. For this reason Mexicans call it the Secret Flower. The buds open slowly, a few at a time, starting at the base. There is a long blooming season and the plant can become very large, up to 12 feet in height with many clusters of flowers.

Candlebush is one of the oldest sources of American medicines, providing cures since the days of Aztecs. Folk medicines for various skin diseases are derived from this plant. The leaves are used in the treatment of ringworm.

Candlebush is grown throughout the tropics and is a wildflower in many places. It is native to the Americas.

Oyster Plant *(Rhoeo spathacea)*

Other common names include Moses-in-the-Bullrushes, and Boat Lily. The small white blooms are almost hidden among the large colorful leaves.

Parts of these plants are used in folk medicine to stop bleeding. Oyster Plant is native to tropical America.

Natal Plum (*Carissa grandiflora*)

The fruit of the Natal Plum is edible, thus proving false the claim that all plants with milky sap are poisonous. The bush makes a very good, impenetrable hedge because of its large and sharp thorns.

Peregrina (*Jatropha integerrima*)

Also known as Spicy Jatropha, it can grow either as a bush or as a tree. It is native to the island of Cuba.

Gardenia *(Gardenia jasminoides)*

The Gardenia has what many consider to be the most wonderful fragrance of any flower. In Hawaii, it is used for some of the most expensive leis. At one time, it was called Cape Jasmine and was thought to have originated in the Cape area of South Africa, but this was later shown to be untrue.

It has been noted that some of the most fragrant flowers (such as Gardenia, Jasmine, and Citrus) are white in color, but the scientific significance of this, if any, is not yet known. It is known that fragrant flowers are usually pollinated by insects.

The Gardenia is from China and is a member of the Coffee family of plants.

Turk's Cap *(Malvaviscus arboreus)*

This Mexican bush very much resembles a Hibiscus whose flowers never quite open. It is sometimes called Sleeping Hibiscus.

In its native Mexico, a sore throat medicine is made from the flowers of this plant.

Coral Plant *(Jatropha multifida)*

The flowers grow in a cluster which resembles red coral. The female flower is at the center with the male flowers grouped around it. The seeds are poisonous if swallowed.

Star Cluster *(Pentas spp.)*

The scientific name comes from a Greek word meaning "five," for five petals. These delicate plants come in a variety of colors. They are rather sensitive to cold weather.

Golden Shrimp Plant
(Pachystachys lutea)

This Peruvian plant was not introduced to growers in this country until 1964.

Lantana *(Lantana camara)*

This plant is common as a wildflower but also popular with gardeners. It is a danger to grazing animals because it is poisonous if eaten. It has spread rapidly and become a pest in some places such as Hawaii.

The various varieties all feature two colors of flowers arranged in an inner and outer ring. As the flowers mature, the colors change, yellow turning to orange and orange to red.

Crown-of-Thorns *(Euphorbia milii)*

The stems are heavily covered with thorns and the tiny flowers are surrounded by colorful red bracts. In legend, this plant was used to make the thorny crown placed on Christ's head at the time of his crucifixion. As part of this story, the red bracts symbolized the drops of His blood.

Scholars now believe that this plant, which is native to Madagascar, was probably unknown to the people of the Bible lands at that time. They speculate that Chist's crown-of-thorns was made from another plant, possibly the Acacia Tree.

Dwarf Poinciana
(Caesalpinia pulcherrima)

    This shrub is grown in tropical countries all over the world. It has been called the Peacock Flower, Pride of Barbados and the Barbados Flower-Fence. It loses its leaves in the winter and can look rather ragged, but more than makes up for it with a fiery display of blooms all spring and summer. The flowers have especially long stamens.

    It is native to the American tropics. In Guatemala, the leaves of the plant are used to stupify fish. In India, an ink is extracted from the wood.

Yesterday, Today, and Tomorrow
(Brunfelsia spp.)

    This shrub produces a lavender colored flower that fades to pure white over a period of several days. As a result it appears that the plant has three kinds of flowers; lavender, white, and an intermediate shade. While the flower is dark in color, it has a ring of white, in the center, like an eye. Another common name is Kiss-Me-Quick (Before-I-Fade).

Impatiens *(Impatiens spp.)*

An interesting feature of this plant is that one petal always has a deep notch. The stamens are united in a small cone shape at the center of the flower. Underneath the flower is a long, tubular spur containing nectar.

The name Impatiens derives from "impatience" because the seeds are expelled from their pods immediately after ripening.

This flower is valuable in landscaping because it grows well in shade, adding a touch of bright color to dark areas of a garden. It is a native of Zanzibar.

Cape Honeysuckle
(Tecomaria capensis)

This rambling South African shrub is very common throughout South Florida. The name is a little misleading, because it belongs to a different family than the true honeysuckles. There is a variety with bright yellow flowers.

The flowers attract hummingbirds in the Americas and sunbirds (the Old World equivalent of hummingbirds) in Africa.

Spathe Flower *(Spathiphyllum spp.)*

The flower cluster, or inflorescence, is guarded by a large white or green-colored leaf-like structure called a "spathe."

Some plants have a white spathe, some green. In still other plants, the spathe changes from white to green as the flower matures.

The young flower spikes are used for food in Central Amercia. In South America, the leaves are added to tobacco for extra aroma.

Firespike *(Odontonema strictum)*

This flower, also known as Red Justicia, is unusual because the many buds open irregularly rather than starting from the top or bottom like most flowers. This gives the flower spike a ragged, but interesting appearance.

*Authors Note: This Spathe Flower was photographed in Costa Rica. It is one of the varieties commonly grown in Florida. But don't hold your breath while looking for this Gaudy Leaf Frog. He is not really appropriate for a Florida book, but I just couldn't resist. This photo won the Natural History Magazine nature photography competition for Libby Lyons. I wish I had taken this shot.

Flame-of-the-Woods (*Ixora* spp.)

This plant produces flowers in ball-shaped clusters. Some varieties produce the flower clusters all over the plant and may be used to create one of the world's most colorful hedges. Unlike many other flowering plants, Ixora may be trimmed into formal shapes without seriously disrupting its heavy blooming.

The name *Ixora* comes from Ishwara, one of the many names for the Hindu god, Shiva. Along India's Malabar Coast, the flowers of certain *Ixora* species are used as temple offerings.

Periwinkle (*Catharanthus roseus*)

Native to Madagascar, this flower has long been useful in folk medicine and recently yielded two important anti-cancer drugs (Vincristine and Vinblastine) which are effective in the treatment of childhood leukemia.

Medical researchers continue to investigate plants known to have been used by tribal healers in the hope of finding other important drugs. In addition to alleviating suffering, drugs derived from Periwinkle alone are worth millions of dollars annually.

Firecracker Plant
(Russelia equisetiformis)

This flashy plant has only a few tiny leaves and blooms almost continuously. Since there is almost no foliage, it produces food along the green surfaces of the stems. It is native to Mexico.

Another common name is Fountain Plant. The many arching stems give it a weeping, fountain-like appearance. It is also called Rain-of-Fire, and Cook's Earrings.

King's Crown *(Justicia carnea)*

The petals of this South American flower have a very distinctive hooded shape.

King's Crown is a relative of the Shrimp Plant. Another common name for this colorful flower is Cardinal's Feather. When grown from seed, the flowers range in color from light pink to deep rose.

In Brazil it is called the Rat Plant because its fruits are mixed with other foods to produce an effective bait for rodents.

Castor Oil Plant *(Ricinus communis)*

This African plant grows wild but is also used as an ornamental shrub. The seeds yield the once popular castor oil which now is valued most for industrial purposes.

The seeds contain a very toxic substance called Ricin. It is not soluble in oil, so, it is not a problem in the production of castor oil. Unfortunately, the seeds are so pretty that they are sometimes strung as necklaces and given to children as playthings. If the seeds are chewed, breaking the hard shell, and then swallowed, the result could be disastrous.

Ricinus means "tick" in Latin. The name derives from the interesting pattern on the seeds which gives them some resemblance to the common tick.

Powderpuff (*Calliandra haematocephala*)

Each bloom is actually many small flowers with inconspicuous, almost invisible petals. The showy part consists of hundreds of long, pollen-tipped stamens, the male flower-parts.

The species Latin name, *haematocephala*, means literally "blood-red head."

Powderpuffs are native to tropics of the Americas.

Pampas Grass (*Cortaderia selloana*)

Pampas Grass grows profusely on the pampas plains of Argentina. Gauchos must wear protective leather leg coverings to prevent cuts when riding through this grass.

In Florida, it blooms in the fall with very showy shoots of fluffy flowers that look a little like cotton candy. The flower clusters of the female plants are larger and more attractive than those of the male plant.

The blooms are grown commercially for dried flower arrangements and the leaves have been used in manufacturing paper.

Pagoda Flower
(Clerodendrum paniculatum)

This ornamental bush is related to the Bleeding Heart and the Glorybower. It is a native of Southeast Asia.

Firethorn *(Pyracantha spp.)*

After flowering in the spring, this bush has lots of fire as its berries ripen in the fall. Care must be used in pruning because flowers and berries are borne only on those stalks that are at least a year old. It is a native of China.

Azalea *(Rhododendron hybrids)*

This flower has been in cultivation for hundreds of years. A native of Java, it was first cultivated in Japan where many new varieties were created.

Certain fungi grow on the roots of Azaleas and may help provide nutrients which the plants could not get from the soil by themselves. This may be one reason the plants prosper in a very acid soil.

Water Lily *(Nymphaea* hybrids*)*

Water lilies are neither bulbs nor lilies, but belong to a more primitive family of flowering plants. The tropical species will bloom all year if the water stays warm. Some species are strictly night blooming. A water garden can bloom 24 hours a day if the proper mixture of species is selected.

The work to produce the fancy modern hybrids began in France 100 years ago, but Water Lilies have been in cultivation far longer. These flowers were placed in the tombs of the ancient Egyptians and were depicted in their hieroglyphics. The Latin name derives from the water nymphs of Greek mythology.

Lisianthus
(Eustoma grandiflorum x Eustoma exaltata)

Lisianthus is a relatively new flower growing in popularity in Florida. It was hybridized by Japanese horticulturists and then introduced to Florida growers in 1983. It features beautiful flowers that are long-lasting when cut for arrangements.

41

FOLIAGE PLANTS

Dumb Cane *(Dieffenbachia* spp.*)*

In brutal times past, slaves in Jamaica were forced to drink the juice of this plant as a punishment. The juice swells the larynx and causes temporary loss of the voice, hence the common name, Dumb Cane.

This plant is easy to root from cuttings and is very common as a houseplant in Florida. Some people are sensitive to the juice touching their skin and care should be used when making cuttings.

Selloum *(Philodendron selloum)*

This very common landscape plant has an interesting pattern of leaf scars on its trunk. Sometimes called Split-Leaf Philodendron, it is native to Brazil.

The name Philodendron comes from Greek words meaning "to love a tree," a reference to the tree-climbing species of this plant.

Croton *(Codiaeum* spp.*)*

Crotons are proof that the bloom is not always the showiest part of a plant. Crotons are native to the South Pacific where they have been used as a symbol of royalty. They were widely distributed through the Pacific islands before the arrival of the Europeans, although the native Crotons were quite different from the plants popular today.

The really flashy colors have been created through hybridizing. Like Hibiscus hybrids, the modern varieties of Croton bear little resemblance to their wild ancestors.

Florida is one of the few places in the United States where Crotons can be grown out-of-doors year-around. There are an enormous number of varieties.

Some of the yellow and green combinations have been called Canned Sunshine because the colors are so brilliant. Another common name is Indian Paintbrush.

Swiss Cheese Plant
(Monstera deliciosa)

This plant can grow as a free-standing shrub or climb onto a support. It produces a white flower spike surrounded by a protective white leaf called a "spathe." It takes over a year for the flower to ripen into a mature fruit.

The leaves are full of holes, like Swiss cheese. Various theories have been presented to explain the function of these holes. Some believe they allow extra light to reach the lower leaves and more water to reach the roots. Some think the function may be to cool the leaf and prevent overheating.

An Unusual Taste Treat! The fruit of Monstera is delicious if eaten properly. When unripe, the fruit contains calcium oxalate crystals which will sting the inside of the mouth painfully. The fruit ripens gradually from the bottom of the stalk. When ripe, the beautifully patterned outer green skin will peel away revealing white fleshy fruit underneath. Only a few inches per day will ripen. Use caution to eat just a little each day and not to eat beyond the point where the skin has peeled up by itself. Do not eat the green skin or fruit attached to it. The fruit is said to have the combined taste of Banana, Strawberry, and Pineapple and thus has been called "everyman's fruit." It actually consists of hundreds of tiny, individual berries joined together. The small photo above shows the ripe fruit ready to eat.

Coleus *(Coleus* hybrids*)*

This member of the Mint family is prized for the beautiful color patterns on its foliage and its velvety soft texture.

Pothos *(Epipremnum aureum)*

Pothos is sometimes called Hunters Robe because natives in the Pacific Islands wrap themselves with the vine for camouflage when hunting in the jungle. It is also called Variegated Philodendron.

Purple Queen *(Setcreasea pallida)*

This native of Mexico is popular as a ground cover. The sap may cause some people to develop a stinging rash.

Ligustrum *(Ligustrum japonicum)*

The pretty, white blooms of this bush are not commonly seen because Ligustrum is most frequently planted as a hedge and all stray sprouts are carefully trimmed off. It is especially common around Palm Beach where high walls created of trimmed Ligustrum protect some of the most expensive homes.

Sometimes called Privet, this plant is native to Japan where it is also popular for use as a privacy hedge.

Elephant Ears
(Xanthosoma, Alocasia, and *Colocasia* spp.*)*

The roots of this plant are cultivated and eaten as a vegetable in parts of the Caribbean, Southeast Asia, and Polynesia. The rhizomes provide a starchy substitute for rice. Careful preparation is necessary. When raw, all parts of this plant contain a stinging poison.

It is one of the most frequently reported causes of plant poisoning in Florida, probably because children are naturally fascinated with the enormous leaves which are large enough to dwarf a man.

Copperleaf *(Acalypha wilkesiana)*

No two leaves are alike on this plant, thus another common name of Match-Me-If-You-Can. It is native to the South Pacific.

Asparagus Fern
(Asparagus densiflorus 'Sprengeri')

This plant is not a fern. Although its foliage is fern-like, it has pretty little white flowers and red berries. It is used as a ground-cover and is related to the edible Asparagus.

Umbrella Plant *(Cyperus alternifolius)*

A close relative of the Papyrus plant, it has been cultivated for hundreds of years in tropical water gardens around the world.

SUCCULENT PLANTS

Succulents in Florida

Florida is not dry, but it does have a warm climate and a number of desert plants are common here. These plants have developed special mechanisms for their survival in dry climates. Succulents have thick, fleshy, water-storing leaves.

Hen and Chickens (*Echeveria* spp.)

The Latin name of this large group of succulent plants honors a famous Mexican botanical artist.

The climate of Mexico and the southwest of the United States is especially favorable for this type of plant, but many species will also grow well in Florida.

Kalanchoe (*Kalanchoe* spp.)

This plant is one of a number of succulents grown for their fascinating appearance. This particular succulent also has beautiful flowers. It is native to Madagascar.

Many people pronounce the name as "Kal-an-cho" but the proper pronunciation is more like "Kal-an-ko-ee."

Prickly Pear *(Opuntia* spp.*)*

The fruit of the Prickly Pear can be eaten or used to make drinks and is sometimes available in Florida grocery stores. This fruit has been called Red Bunny Ears.

The founding of Mexico City is associated with this plant. According to the legend, the Aztec priests saw an eagle sitting on a Prickly Pear Cactus and strangling a snake. Interpreting this as a sign of victory over their tribal enemies, they decided to stay at this particular location and Mexico City was born.

This colorful story is illustrated on the flag of Mexico.

Snake Plant *(Sansevieria* spp.*)*

This popular plant is also known as Mother-in-Law's Tongue. It is raised commercially in many countries for fiber used to make string, nets, and fabric. In Africa, the string from this fiber is used for hunting bows, hence another common name, Bowstring Hemp.

Snake Plants have even been called the "donkeys of the houseplants" for their ability to withstand bad treatment from their owners.

Prickly Pear

Snake Plant

Moss Rose detail

Spanish Bayonet *(Yucca aloifolia)*

The leaves of this plant are very stiff and very sharp-pointed. They are capable of inflicting painful puncture wounds if a person is careless enough to stumble against them. For safety's sake, some homeowners have covered their sharp tips with ping-pong balls or even pieces of styrofoam egg cartons. The result is a little bit silly-looking.

The beautiful white flowers are fragrant at night. The flower petals are edible, and while slightly bitter tasting, are an unusual addition to raw salads. A native of Mexico, and possibly Florida, this plant is common along the coastline on both sides of the state.

Moss Rose *(Portulaca grandiflora)*

The Moss Rose is neither a moss nor a rose. It is a beautiful, flowering succulent plant frequently used as a groundcover.

American Indians crushed the seeds and used the powder to make a mush. The method for easily collecting the seeds in quantity was to stack up large piles of the plant and then, a few days later, gather all the seeds that had fallen underneath.

Aloe *(Aloe saponaria)*

Aloe is an ornamental succulent native to African deserts. In Africa, Aloe is believed to drive away evil spirits and is used around homes and cemeteries as protection against supernatural dangers.

It is of considerable interest in Florida for its healthful juices. A gel made from this plant is popular as a skin lotion for moisturizing and for relief of burns. It is even taken by some as a health-giving beverage.

The species most commonly used in commercial production is Aloe Vera. Aloe Vera means "true aloe." It is so named because, of the 200 species of Aloe, the Aloe Vera plant produces the largest amount of the active ingredient, "aloin."

Aloe is frequently mentioned in the Bible. The Aloe species is said to have been planted by the Lord himself (Numbers 24:6). The shroud of Jesus was prepared with a mixture of Myrrh and Aloes (John 19:39). Here are some other Bible references: Song of Solomon 4:14, Psalms 45:8, Proverbs 7:17.

Century Plant *(Agave* spp.*)*

The name Century Plant is given to this desert grower because it was once thought that it would flower only when it reached the age of one hundred. Actually, it can bloom after only seven to ten years. The blooming is still something quite special and once it does flower, the plant dies.

The blooms occur on a stem which can be 35 feet tall. The growth of the stem is very rapid, up to 5 inches or more per day, but even so, it takes many weeks to reach the full height. The stalk of the bloom will remain on the plant for months. The Agave will have produced suckers before blooming, so new plants will arise as the old plant dies.

In addition, small yet complete baby plants, called "bulbils," form at the top of the bloom stalk. They are not the result of fruit germinating, but more like detachable suckers. When these plants fall to the ground, even more new Agaves will appear.

3:00 PM

5:30 PM

9:00 AM

Weeks Later

Mahoe *(Hibiscus tiliaceus)*

The Mahoe is common in south Florida landscaping and prospers along the coastline. It generally produces flowers all year. The flowers open bright yellow in the morning and gradually darken to a deep red by the end of the day before finally wilting. This one-day bloom schedule is common but not strictly true. Some blooms mature more slowly and remain on the tree for more than a day.

Beach Naupaka *(Scaevola frutescens)*

Naupaka is a succulent plant which prospers along the beaches. It is native to Asia and has beautiful white berries and small white flowers which always appear to be torn in half.

There is a legend which tells of a young couple who quarreled. The angry woman tore a Naupaka flower in half and told her lover she would not speak to him again until he brought her a perfect replacement. He searched diligently, but in vain. All the flowers of the Naupaka had become halves and he died of a broken heart.

Sea Grape *(Coccoloba uvifera)*

This Florida native plant thrives in sandy beach environments. Its most striking features are the circular leaves with red veins and the large clusters of fruit which appear in the summer and ripen to a dark color in the fall. The fruit appears in abundance only on the female trees while the male trees will show just the dead flower spikes.

The fruit is used to make wine and jelly. The "grapes" do not ripen together as a cluster, but individually, at different times.

Sea Oats *(Uniola paniculata)*

These grasses grow along coastal areas from Virginia to Texas. The attractive seed heads form at the end of the summer and remain on the plant for months.

Sea Oats are very valuable for stabilizing sand dunes and beach areas. They prevent beach erosion through their elaborate root structure. Once popular for dried flower arrangements, they are now protected by Florida statute and it is unlawful to pick them.

GINGERS

Gingers look like small Bamboo plants with leaves that are generally blade-shaped. They are distant relatives of the Banana and can range in height from a few feet up to giants over fifteen feet tall.

Some gingers are grown for spice and perfume, others are just ornamental. The ginger root sold in grocery stores, *Zingiber officinale*, can be planted in Florida gardens. It will grow here and might even flower.

Shell Ginger (*Alpinia zerumbet*)

This plant bears shiny, porcelain-like sprays of flowers in the spring and summer. In Asia where it is native, the plant is used for fiber and paper production.

White Ginger (*Hedychium coronarium*)

This flower has a wonderful fragrance, especially at night. It is used in perfume making and for Hawaiian leis. It is also known as Butterfly Lily or Ginger Lily.

The small photos from left show Pine Cone Ginger, Costus and Red Ginger.

HELICONIAS

Heliconias are from Central and South America and from the Old World tropics ("Old World" means the eastern hemisphere). They were at one time classified with the Banana family, but now have their own family. Natives in South America use the leaves for food, but in the United States Heliconias are grown for their beauty in gardens.

The showiest part of these plants are the formations of colorful bracts surrounding the flowers. The actual flowers are usually small and inconspicuous.

BROMELIADS

Most bromeliads are epiphytes (epi meaning "upon" and phyte meaning "plant"). They grow on trees, but they are not parasites, and they do not derive any nourishment from the trees. In many bromeliads, the leaves form a cup or container in the center of the plant which is called a "tank."

The tank collects water and insects. The plant derives nourishment from organic matter which falls into the tank. The roots can also take in water and nourishment, but they are small and used mostly for support. The bromeliad depends mainly on the tank for nourishment.

Some bromeliads grow on the ground (such as the Pineapple) but most grow in trees. After flowering and producing seeds, the bromeliad will die, but offshoots called "pups" will grow in its place.

The photo at the top of this page is *Neoregelia carolinae*; at left, *Neophytum* 'Ralph Davis'; at the top of the opposite page, *Aechmea* spp.

A Hard Life

Air-plants (such as the bromeliads which live in trees) have no roots in contact with moist soil. It is difficult for them to retain moisture during the dry season. How they manage to do it is not completely understood, but it is now known that they utilize a metabolism that is different from other plants.

Most plants take in the carbon dioxide they need for food production during the daytime by opening the pores (stomates) on their leaves, but this results in loss of water. Most air-plants are able to take in carbon dioxide at night and then store it for daytime use. By not opening their pores during the heat of the day, they conserve much valuable moisture.

Billbergia *(Billbergia pyramidalis)*

This "bromel" (as bromeliads are sometimes called by those who grow them) is known as the Fool-Proof Plant because it is easy to grow and frost resistant. The spectacular blooms occur in the late summer.

FERNS

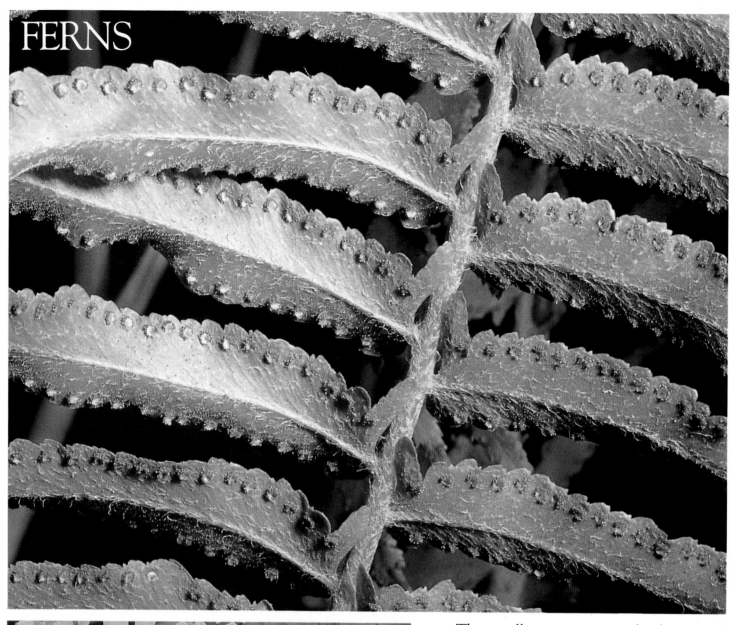

The small spots seen on the bottom of most fern leaves are called sori. If you look at these spots with a magnifier, you will see that each is really a cluster of tiny spore cases. The spore cases are called sporangia.

Spores do not become plants easily, which may be why nature produces them in enormous quantities. When the spore cases burst open, the spores are sprayed into the air like a powder.

Ancient peoples knew about spore dust and thought it had magic qualities. They believed it would make them invulnerable to their enemies and increase their powers as great lovers, among other benefits. They ate it, drank it, and poured it over themselves.

Maidenhair Fern (Adiantum spp.)

These ferns need cool and moist conditions and are not so common because they are hard to grow. In Roman mythology, this fern represents the hair of Venus, goddess of love and beauty.

Staghorn Fern *(Platycerium spp.)*

Whole books have been written on just the varieties of Staghorn. They need no soil but will grow on the bark of trees in nature. Water from rain and nutrients such as bird droppings or dead insects are funneled to the root system by specially designed leaves. The base of the fern is like a head of cabbage and has specialized leaves (called "sterile leaves") which protect the root system. Only the outer leaves will bear the spores.

Hare's Foot *(Polypodium spp.)*

This fern has an interesting furry structure resembling a rabbit's foot. This "foot" is a rhizome which is a kind of creeping stem responsible for new growth. Other "footed ferns" have been called Bear's Paw, Squirrel's Foot and other animal names.

Close relatives of these ferns are frequently found growing wild in Florida's Cabbage Palms. Unfortunately, ferns found growing in the wild sometimes do not adapt as well to life as houseplants as those raised in a greenhouse and bred for that purpose.

BULBOUS PLANTS

Caladium *(Caladium bicolor)*

This plant from tropical America has beautiful leaves which open in the summer and die back in the winter. It is a member of the Aroid family. Large commercial nurseries near Lake Placid grow many varieties for Florida gardeners and for shipment throughout the United States.

Caladiums are sometimes mistakenly referred to as bulbs, but are actually tubers. The beautiful foliage of the Caladium has earned the plant the name Artist's Palette.

The bright colors of the leaves play a part in the pollination strategy of this plant. The flowers of Caladium are not very showy but low-flying or crawling insects looking up through the leaves see what botanists call a "stained-glass window" effect. They are attracted to the bright colors and are thus led to the flowers.

African Iris *(Dietes spp.)*

True irises are native to the northern hemisphere while these very similar plants come from the southern hemisphere, primarily the region of South Africa.

Canna *(Canna indica)*

The Canna is native to tropical America (including Florida) and also Asia.

The colorful parts of the flower that look like petals are actually modified stamens. The real petals are small and greenish-colored.

The hard black seeds have been used for Buddhist rosaries. The word Canna means "help from Buddha."

Blood Lily *(Haemanthus spp.)*

Each cluster will contain 50 to 100 individual flowers. It is native to Africa. *Haemanthus* means "blood flower."

Society Garlic *(Tulbaghia violacea)*

Some people believe planting Society Garlic in gardens will help keep insects away from surrounding plants because of the odor of its leaves which resembles garlic or onions. It may ward off some pests such as mites and scales, but probably would not defend against anything as aggressive as a grasshopper.

Society Garlic may have been so named because the beautiful flowers make the plant socially acceptable in spite of its garlic smell.

COLLECTOR SPECIALTY PLANTS

The balmy warm climate of South Florida makes possible the cultivation of many interesting and beautiful exotics. These are a few of the many fantastic plants that can be grown here but are not readily available.

Dutchman's Pipe
(Aristolochia gigantea)

This unique flower has an efficient insect trap. There is a pouch with a small opening. Inside the pouch, one area of the wall is very thin and admits light easily.

The insect that has entered the pouch is lured to the light. It is here that the pollen is located. (photo is top, right)

Flamingo Flower
(Anthurium andraeanum)

The flowers are tiny and packed together on a colorful spike surrounded by a heart-shaped bract ranging in color from white to pink to deep red.

The colorful bracts sometimes turn green, revealing their origins as leaves.

(photo is bottom, right)

Medinilla *(Medinilla magnifica)*

This beautiful shrub comes from the rain forests of the Philippines (photo is top, left).

Bolivian Sunset *(Gloxinia sylvatica)*

This plant is a recent introduction from Bolivia and a sample of some of the beautiful plants that are available from other countries but not yet popularized here (bottom, left).